p_1

"At its very root, Christianity is not about religion, but relationship. By giving us a window into her own relationship with Jesus Christ, Lori invites us to know more deeply the person, power and grace of Jesus for ourselves. Read and find life here!"

—Corey Widmer, Lead Pastor, Third Church

"Dallas Willard once remarked that, "On the other side of complexity is simplicity." It is not always easy to sort through the complexities of life in ways that identify the nuggets on the other side. Lori Booker has a talent for distilling the great devotional truths of the spiritual life into ways that help us grasp and apply them to our own lives in a simple and practical manner ..."

—Pastor David "Tuck" Knupp

"I love having Lori as a friend, and one thing I know about her is that she loves people! That is evident in this book, as she writes with honesty, humility, and joy, while telling us about her favorite Friend-Jesus. This book is fun to read. As you get to know Lori, I believe it also fulfills her great desire—that anyone who reads this book would be introduced to Jesus or be encouraged to love Him more than ever before."

—Faye Rivers, Teaching Director Community Bible Study, over 20 years

marked

& sealed

a journal of God's loving pursuit

LORI FARRAR BOOKER

MARKED AND SEALED

www.lorifarrarbooker.com

9781092374309
Printed in the United States of America.

DEDICATION

Dedication is defined as devotion, with persistent effort and time poured into a particular someone, something, or purpose. It means allegiance that is constant, devout, unswerving, loyal and truehearted.

I can think of no other than the Lord Himself that is devoted in this manner. People shift and lose heart, but He is never changing, always faithful and true.

And so, without further ado, I dedicate this book to Him.

His fingerprints mark and seal every page.
His fingerprints are everywhere along the way.
Every page is dedicated to Him.
And what's more—He's dedicated to us!

CONTENTS

FOREWORD

I am marked with struggles, flaws, aches and regrets.
I am sealed with joy, victory, forgiveness and peace.
I am found.

My life is a story of God's pursuing love through many twists and turns. He has never failed me and has loved me through it all. Each page of this journal marks another instance of His enduring presence coming to my side, showering me with His tender grace and mercy along the road. He reminds me that I am accepted and never alone. He covers me and cares for me, settles me and holds me, loves me and leads me, strengthens and encourages me. He simply amazes me.

He shows up in unexpected ways in my ordinary days. He has a way with touching my moments, confirming His desire for me to know Him and to live a life in Him. These journal pages are filled with just a few of His many loving pursuits, extending and revealing His trusted hand. It is beautiful—the way He gently carries me and steals my heart. Has He stolen yours?

As you turn the pages, consider what He might be wanting to show you. Take the time to pause and use the blank pages to personally ponder. Mark them as your own.

Be captured by His unfailing love and grace.

Marked and Sealed,

NICE TO MEET YOU

When I was young, I had a journal.
It was the kind that came with a lock.
I was the only one who held the key.
You can be sure I didn't want anybody seeing what it was that
I had scratched on those pages.
There are some things you just don't want anybody to know.

The same is true when you first meet a person.
You usually don't tell them the secret things of your heart.
It takes time together and intentionality to form a bond
that is trustworthy.
Even then, there's a tendency to be on guard.
There's the fear of being judged and rejected.
It takes courage.

I'm no different, I'm warming up to the idea of sharing my
deepest struggles, aches and regrets. I wanted to let you know
who I am and where I'm coming from. I am marked with a
wandering heart that has scars. I don't have it altogether, I
just know the One who does, my Savior—Jesus.

He has read all of my pages and didn't reject me, but accepted me. This is why I have such an urgency in my heart to introduce you to Him. I want to point you to the One who receives secrets, mends hearts and changes your whole world.

He has sealed my whole heart and has delivered me into peace, joy, forgiveness and victory.

I'm looking forward to spending time with you.
Let's unlock this journal and uncover His secrets.
Let me show you the One who is reliable,
approachable and present.

Be taken by Him.
Lean in close and hear the steady rhythm of His heart that beats for us.

Just always remember where I'm coming from, weakness and rescue.
He is my strength and my song.

Nice to meet you.

COME ON IN

Ask and it will be given to you,
seek and you will find,
knock and the door will be
opened to you,
for everyone who asks receives,
the one who seeks finds,
and to the one who knocks,
the door will be opened.

Matthew 7:7-8

COME ON IN

It always strikes me when I travel down this windy road at the river and see the infamous house with the front door that sits up high. There are no stairs to the door. What is this? Nobody could ever make it to their door to knock. It is such a mystery to me as to why they haven't taken the time to put stairs in. In fact, it's kind of cold-looking from the outside—nothing inviting about it at all.

What if I wanted to visit? It would feel strange to go around back since I don't know them. I would only want to go to the front door, but how would I get there?

Maybe you don't know the Lord yet and it seems strange to approach Him, let alone to visit Him. Let me assure you. There are sturdy stairs in place and you can make it to His front door. You can feel free and without worry to go right on up and knock. He's taken the time to make His door accessible. He has been expecting you and is lovingly waiting for you on the other side. He will gladly open it and welcome you in!

You are invited. There are blooming spring flowers out front, a welcome flag blows in the wind by the door, and the doormat reads *Home Sweet Home*. Once you're inside, you will never want to leave. You can be sure that He will invite you to stay and, something tells me, you'll gladly accept.

Lord, thank You that we can reach You. You are approachable and You desire that we come and knock and find You. You will most certainly unlock the mysteries of life to us when we decide to seek.
You want us to find You.

Come on in!

ENJOY THE RIDE

Be still and know
that He is God.

Psalm 46 : 10

ENJOY THE RIDE

I clutch the car door handle, my knuckles are white. I suck in the air in panic and intently watch all the vehicles around us, offering input to keep us from getting into an accident. I'm looking forward to reaching the airport and exiting the passenger door with my life intact. I will then wait to board the plane and feel anxious as I prepare to place my life in the hands of the pilot.

It's hard not being in control.
Can you relate?
Why do I want to be in the driver's seat instead?

Control is defined as the power
to influence the course of events.

I "white knuckle it" too much. My power of influence is so limited within myself, the overriding power comes from God. When I quiet my heart and release my grip, it brings deep peace, joy and relief.

Be still and know that He is God.
Let Him drive and enjoy the ride!

TRUST FALL

Trust in the Lord with all your heart,
lean not on your own understanding,
acknowledge Him in all your ways
and He will make your paths straight.

Proverbs 3 : 5-6

TRUST FALL

You have likely played the game before.
Someone stands behind you.
You plant your feet in one place
and leave them there.
You then fall back with all your weight.
You are trusting that person to catch you.

I am usually hesitant.
I look at the person more than once
to be sure they are ready.

On this particular day,
I was supposed to catch the person.
Now he was much bigger than me
but, I assured him,
I was ready and was up for the challenge.

Ready 1-2-3.

Oh, he trusted me alright. He fell back full force.
I failed to catch him,
and we both fell to the ground laughing.
I couldn't catch him, as hard as I tried.

The truth is ...
There is someone there to catch us.
We can fall back, we don't need to hesitate.
He is much bigger than we are.
It is no challenge to Him.
He is ready.
He will never fail us.
He will always catch us.

Fall into His arms.
Trust Jesus with all your heart.

Ready 1-2-3!

ZIP MY LIP

Do not let any unwholesome talk
come out of your mouths,
but only what is helpful for building others up
according to their needs,
that it may benefit those who listen.

Ephesians 4 : 29

ZIP MY LIP

Sometimes I wish I had a zipper for my lips. When I felt the wrong words building up, I could just reach up and pull the zipper closed.

XYZPDQ

A friend of mine used to say,
"What's down in the well comes up in the bucket."
In other words, what's in our hearts comes out of
our mouths!

Words are so revealing.

"For whatever is in your heart determines what you say."
(Matthew 12:34)

It all starts in the heart. The heart, a secret place in each of us, but a place not hidden from Jesus. He knows our deepest struggles and we can invite Him in to examine our hearts, to mend the hard and hurt places, and to begin to transform the very words that come out of our mouths.

Once the toothpaste is out of the tube, can you put it back in?

And so it is with our words, you can't put them back either.

Words either build up or tear down.

"Gracious words are a honeycomb, sweet to the soul." (Proverbs 16:24)

Lord, search our hearts and mend our hurts— fill our buckets. Give us gracious words that benefit the listener, sweet to our souls and theirs."

XYZPDQ

NO HIDING

Then the man and his wife
heard the sound of the Lord God
as he was walking in the garden
in the cool of the day
and they hid from the Lord God
among the trees of the garden
but the Lord God called to the man,
"Where are you?"

Genesis 3 : 8-9

NO HIDING

Our puppy dog is smart.
So smart that he knows how to play hide and go seek.
We pick a good place to hide.
We then beg the question, "Where is "so & so"?
Even if more than one of us is hiding,
he finds the very one whose name we called aloud.
It's quite amazing.
He knows us by name and finds us every time.
Once he spots us, the tail starts wagging a mile a minute.
You can see him smile.

We are good at hiding and so were Adam and Eve.
You have heard the story about them?
They were the ones in the garden.
They ate the forbidden apple, remember?
From deep within, they knew they had done wrong,
And guess what they did?

They hid.

Does this sound familiar?
The apple doesn't fall so far from the tree.

Here's what we need to remember ...
God immediately called out in the garden,
"Adam, where are you?"

Adam hid, we hide,
but God always knows where we are,
and He calls out in love, "Where are you?"
He wants us to come out from hiding
and be found by Him.

"Where are you?"

Answer Him—He's quite amazing.
He knows you by name and will welcome you every time.
Rest assured, His arms will be open and He will be smiling.

There's no need to hide.

H - E - L - P

I lift my eyes to the hills,
from where does my help come?
My help comes from the Lord,
the maker of heaven and earth.

Psalm 121 : 1-2

H - E - L - P

They stood at the altar to seal their vows.
As they knelt together at the altar for the final blessings,
the crowd began to chuckle among themselves.
It was the bottom of the groom's shoes.
His friends had inscribed H-E on one shoe, L-P on the other.
There in plain view it read "HELP"!

It was meant as a joke and they still tell the story.
It is funny and it is true.
We do need help.

My husband's shoes didn't reveal anything,
but we have experienced the truth revealed in this story.

It was a typical night, our regular routine.
The kids were sound asleep.
We were wide awake.
They were just babies and so were we.

Crawling through our days,
we were still fragile and learning how to navigate life
as mommy and daddy, husband and wife.

It was that night that we took our first really big step.

We had voiced our goodnights
and lay there in the pitch dark.
You could hear a pin drop.
My eyes were wide open as I stared at the ceiling.
My heart stirred until the words filled my lips
and spilled out.

"Can we pray?" I quietly whispered.
Without hesitation, my husband gently grabbed my hand.
I cried out a brief heartfelt prayer.
It broke the silence and rose past the ceiling.
It filled the ears of the Almighty.

The Lord heard. The Lord hears.

"In my distress I called to the Lord; I cried to my God for help. From His temple He heard my voice; my cry came before Him, into His ears."
(Psalm 18:6)

Have you broken the silence? Have you cried out?

> We come crawling.
> He helps us to stand, to walk and to run.

Write this on your heart—
this is where our help comes from.

Praise You Almighty God. You are our strength and hope in the hills and the valleys. Maker of heaven and earth, we cry out to You continually and stand in awe of your abounding love and constant help. Amen.

SCARED OF THE DARK

Do not be afraid
for I am with you.

Isaiah 43 : 5

SCARED OF THE DARK

When I was a little girl, I can remember waking in the middle of the night. The house would feel so eerie, the stillness, the dead quiet.

It was as if the whole world was asleep.

I was too scared to come out from under the covers. I definitely wouldn't think of going out in the dark hallway.

I'd take a deep breath and my voice would break the silence. I'd scream. "Mom!" "Mom!" It was intentional, holding her name steady and drawn out. I'd repeat this refrain until she came to my rescue.

She'd lovingly show up at my bedside.
She'd take me by the hand and lead me in the dark.
She'd return me back under the covers and comfort me.

I am still scared of the dark.

The house this morning was dead quiet.
The sun was up, but I was down.
I stood peering out the window, a little hopeless.
Scared of not knowing what lies ahead, my thoughts battled, trying to make sense of current life circumstances.
I was struggling to throw off doubt and find peace.
Scared of the unknown.
Scared of the dark.

The Lord came to my rescue and broke through the silence, taking me by the hand ...

"I go before you and will be with you; I will never leave you nor forsake you. Do not be afraid; do not be discouraged." (Deuteronomy 31:8)

Did you know?
The Bible says "Do not be afraid" 365 times.
That's once for each day.
This tells me the Lord has us tagged and He has us covered.

Today He says, "Do not be afraid."
Tomorrow He will remind us again.

> Take a deep breath.
> Let your voice break the silence.
> Call out to Him intentionally.
> "He who watches over you will not slumber."
> (Psalm 121:3)
> He will come to your side,
> take your hand and never let go.
> He lights the way.

"Have I not commanded you? Be strong and courageous. Do not be afraid; do not be discouraged, for the Lord your God will be with you wherever you go." (Joshua 1:9)

We don't have to be scared of the dark!

MY SONG, YOUR SONG

The only thing that counts
is faith expressing itself through love.

Galatians 5 : 6

MY SONG, YOUR SONG

It's early in the morning.
I sit in the quiet listening to the birds.
They sing out with all they have.
Creation shouts a love song in praise for this new day.

I hear what seems to be a chorus from a bird.
It sings its tune over and over, increasingly louder,
fuller, stronger.
It is beautiful.

What song will I sing today?
Will it shout praise?
Will it be beautiful?

The birds are reminding me how to sing.
Love is the key. Love is the tempo.

I hear what seems to be the truth of the matter and the
truth strikes me—
my song has been running low on love.

"Apart from love, I am only a resounding gong
or a clanging cymbal."
(1 Corinthians 13:1)

What song will I sing today?
What song will you sing?

Assist us, Lord, to make music to Your ears
whether it be on a high or low note. Be our vision.
Bring out your song in our hearts. Help us to sing this tune
over and over with all that we have.

Lord, "make Your love increase in us that it might overflow
to others." (1 Thessalonians 3:12)

Your Love be the key. Your Love be the tempo.
Louder, fuller, stronger—My Song, Your Song.

All Praise to You.

Sing! Sing! Sing!

ETERNAL INVESTMENT

Don't store up treasures
here on earth,
where moths eat them
and rust destroys them,
and where thieves break in and steal.
Store your treasures in heaven,
where moths and rust cannot destroy, and
thieves do not break in and steal.
Wherever your treasure is, there the desires
of your heart will also be.

Matthew 6 : 19-21

ETERNAL INVESTMENT

Home decor and renovation are the rage.

Watch *Fixer Upper, Design on a Dime*; pick your favorite show. We invest in the latest designs and treasures.

I have been there, done that.

It was the middle of the day as I drove my regular route.
I spotted signs for an estate sale nearby and decided to go.
I entered the front door to a room full of people and stuff.
I paused ...

As I took in the moment, my heart took in the truth.

I was taken by the emptiness that was there.
The person who had filled that house was gone.
Left behind were all these things covered in dust.
These things couldn't talk, they were lifeless.

I never knew the lady, but I knew that she was gone and
her things were all left behind.

There's nothing wrong with creating a warm home.
We need some things, it is good to have the things
we need.

It becomes not so good when we give things too much attention.

"But godliness with contentment is great gain. For we brought nothing into the world, and we can take nothing out of it." (1 Timothy 6:6-7)

> Things are temporary.
> Our souls are eternal.

We need to treasure the eternal over the temporary.
It is here we find contentment.
We don't take anything with us when we leave this place.
Investing in the eternal has far greater value.

Are you making a good return on your investment?

*Lord Jesus, may we honor You and invest our lives in lasting treasure—**You**. Amen.*

THE BUZZ

Great is our Lord,
and of great power;
His understanding
is infinite.

Psalm 147 : 5

THE BUZZ

To infinity and beyond!
Can you name the voice behind this catch phrase?
It's the one and only Buzz-Lightyear.
Toy Story was the buzz when our kids were young.

Infinity is limitless or endless, impossible to measure.

Can you really go beyond infinity?
I mean, infinity is endless already!
That's a stretch, Buzz!

It seemed I had a limitless view from the plane window.
I gazed out over the city of Richmond.
We were coming in for the landing.
I could see things I never see from ground view.
I liked seeing the bigger picture, but I could only see so far.

I had a plane view,
But God has a PLAIN view.
My view is limited.
God's view is complete.

His understanding is boundless.
Tenderly comprehending every part of us.
His awareness, proficiency and insight,
boundless and inexhaustible.
He knows all ...

"Indeed, the very hairs of your head are all numbered.
Don't be afraid." (Luke 12:7)

You just don't understand.
You are right. I don't, but God does.
Not a best friend or a spouse has understanding of
this magnitude.

"Do you not know? Have you not heard?
The Lord is the everlasting God, the creator of the ends of
the earth. He will not grow tired or weary, and
His understanding no one can fathom."
(Isaiah 40:28)

To infinity and beyond!
He can really go there.
Our One and Only, Great and Powerful Lord.
It's not a stretch for Him.

We can fully trust this kind of understanding.
He sees the bigger picture.
Beyond infinity ...

This is the real buzz!

PAST, PRESENT, FUTURE

Holy, Holy, Holy
is the Lord God Almighty
who was, and is, and is to come!

Revelation 4:8

PAST, PRESENT, FUTURE

What did I do last week?
To be honest, I can only recall but so much.
I fly into one day and out to another.
I wake to the next day and do it all over again.
Yes, there are highlights to each day
that I take away,
but more often than not, I speed through
and miss many details.

You too?

Although we may live and forget,
NOTHING is missed by the Lord, no nothing!
Nothing we do, say or think.
Nothing He planned since the beginning.
He lives and is in all the details.

The sun rises and the sun sets each day,
a picture of His constant hand.
The ocean waves roll onto the shore and back out again.
The promises He made never change.
Each breath we take is from Him.

Just as sure as He was in the beginning,
He is with us now and always will be.

Our past mistakes,
our present worries,
all our sorrows and joys,
our future inheritance in heaven—

He forgets nothing, promises everything and can be trusted
today, tomorrow and forever.

Holy, Holy, Holy,
He Was, and Is, and Is to Come!

*Lord, may we invite You into the present, trust You with
our past and anticipate our forever future held and
secured by You through faith. You are holy and most
worthy of our praise. Amen.*

GET OFF THE BUS

Make every effort
to live in peace with everyone
and to be holy;
without holiness
no one will see the Lord.
See to it that no one falls short
of the grace of God
and that no bitter root grows up
to cause trouble and defile many.

Hebrews 12 : 14-15

GET OFF THE BUS

Remember the days of riding the school bus?
Or maybe you never did.
You've likely taken a charter bus
or some kind of bus, though.
There are many ways to travel.
Bus, car, train, plane—
Some are better than others.

I have taken a train, but only once that I can recall.
I didn't go far.
But, I've taken the bus probably too far.

It's called the "Bitter Bus".
A friend of mine tagged this term and shared it years back.
She reminded me that I choose whether or not I will board.
I laughed aloud and told her that I was the driver.

Honesty is a good policy, but reality says this isn't funny.

Anger, disappointment and resentment ... this is bitterness.
Bitterness wrecks and tarnishes, impairs and destroys.
We can't see the Lord when we are in this state.
It sucks the life out of us. There's nothing sweet about it.

It not only obstructs our vision,
but blocks the view for others.
God's grace is missed.
It can defile many.

Defile?
That paints a picture of ruin; poisoned, spoiled
and polluted.

Defile many?
I would never think of poisoning anyone, let alone many.
I am guilty though of doing so, when I choose the
"Bitter Bus".

We can't begin to see the Light or be the Light when we
choose this ride.

God's ride is much better.
Would you like to join me?
Let's travel only by way of grace.
All aboard!

*Lord, help us to make every effort to get rid of all
bitterness and to live in peace. Help us instead to be
rooted in love; sweet, pleasant and full of You. Amen.*

MY HERO

He is before all things
and in Him
all things hold together.

Colossians 1 : 17

MY HERO

It was a private school entrance exam, time to assess our child's readiness for kindergarten, to measure his intelligence and his capacity to reason. We were there on time and they took our six-year-old son into his assigned testing room. The woman had tested many boys in her day.

It came to a series of questions. She'd state a word and it would spark a relatable logical response. She'd say "fruit". The child would say something like "apple". Then it happened. She said "hero". Our son confidently answered "goddess". What did our son say? Superman, Batman, maybe Spiderman. But "goddess"? Really? Uh-oh, not the right answer!

That night I tucked him in unaware of the story. We were away with family and I went back downstairs. It was then I heard about this happening. The woman doing the testing knew my mother-in-law. She was puzzled and maybe a little concerned with our son's answer and shared the details with my mother-in-law, who proceeded to share.

My heart immediately leapt with conviction. I quickly went upstairs and quietly knelt by our son and softly spoke. "Hey, Buddy, when the lady said "hero" to you today, what did you say?"

Without hesitation, he replied. "I told her ... **GOD IS.**"

Oh, he knew the answer alright, the answer many of us are still missing. This still melts my heart.

A hero is one who inspires you by his actions, is admired for courage, outstanding achievements and noble qualities.
Superman and all his buddies are not the real deal. Our son knew they couldn't hold a candle to our Ultimate Hero. Does God inspire you like this? Do you know Him deeply as your hero?

Superman is faster than a speeding bullet, more powerful than a locomotive, and leaps tall buildings in a single bound, but he has nothing on God.

Heroes suffer for their cause and Jesus suffered for the greatest cause ... "He was delivered over to death for our sins and raised to life for our justification." (Romans 4:25)
Jesus came to save the day!

Our Superhero didn't wear a cape, but wore a cross.
Our Superhero didn't stay in the grave, but rose again.
Our Superhero reigns and holds everything together.

"The Alpha and Omega, the Almighty." (Revelation 1:8)

> He is the beginning
> and the end
> and everything in between.

> Is He your Hero?

WORRY WART

Look at the birds of the air;
they do not sow or reap
or store away in barns,
and yet your heavenly Father
feeds them.
Are you not much more
valuable than they?
Can any one of you by worrying
add a single hour to your life?

Matthew 6 : 26-27

WORRY WART

A worry wart is defined as a person who tends to dwell
unduly on difficulty or troubles.
Often referred to as unsettled and uneasy,
restless and rattled.

Worrying doesn't add anything to our lives,
it only takes away.
It robs us of peace and even thankfulness.
It steals joy and creates doubt.
It doesn't add a single hour to our lives.
Worry steals away our time.

Are you a worry wart?

I admit—I have mastered this title.
Maybe you too?

Look up at the birds freely flying about.
See His tender care for each one.
Know how much more He loves us.

It's time we stop flapping our wings in worry.
We are going nowhere.

Let's instead start moving our lips in prayer and praise.
We will start to take flight.
We will find ourselves soaring above our worries.
Prayer is the wind beneath our wings.

Lord, increase our faith.
Help us to trust You with all the details of our lives.
You hold this world together,
You can hold our lives together too!

OBSESSED

Yet when I surveyed
all that my hands had done
and what I had toiled to achieve
everything was meaningless,
a chasing after the wind.

Ecclesiastes 2 : 11

OBSESSED

There's a song I love called *Be My Magnificent Obsession*. When it plays, I sing it out with all my heart, but when the rubber meets the road, I sing a different song. Before I know it, I become all too obsessed with other things, things that pale in comparison. I'm always striving to finish the to-do list before getting to the more important stuff. Guess what? The list always grows, and well, if I'm not careful, I miss out on what counts most.

Most recently I found myself barking orders at my daughter to clean her room. I could have simply sat among the mess to ask about her day, but I missed the opportunity.

You could tag me a little obsessive. Honestly, we are all prone to this in one area of our lives or another. Your hang-ups may look different than mine, but the result is the same.

Have you ever considered that perhaps we were made to be obsessed with something?

I'm convinced instead of something, it's SOMEONE.
His name is Jesus.

If our hearts are not set on the right thing,
it's a chasing after the wind and we miss out.

Lord, set us free from chasing after the wind. Free us to chase You and the things that matter most. May we sit among the mess and set aside the list to take time with You and with others. Be our Magnificent Obsession. Amen.

NO KIDDING

Be kind and compassionate
to one another,
forgiving each other,
just as in Christ God forgave you.

Ephesians 4 : 32

NO KIDDING

It's still fresh in my mind, even though it was years ago. I was hurt deeply over some words spoken to me that cut me to the core. It was so sudden and caught me off guard, out of nowhere. I had been attacked and couldn't begin to understand why. I calmly responded and told the person how much it hurt me. There was really no response as I remember it. They held their ground and left my presence without closure.

Whoever tagged the saying that "words can never hurt" was all wrong.

What could I do? I wanted to hide, to argue my side, to build a wall between us. How could I forgive someone who had wronged me and hurt me like this? I mean, this person didn't even seem to care that they had done so. There was no apology or even acknowledgement.

And then it happened ...I had an overwhelming thought that wouldn't leave me. *What's that I hear? Make them dinner? You've got to be kidding! Lord, that can't be you telling me to do such a foolish thing!*

I tried to push away this thought, and the more I did, the more I couldn't resist.

I delivered spaghetti dinner the next day. This person wasn't there on my arrival and I can't remember if I heard from them or not. I do know that I never heard the words *I'm sorry*, but I gained so much more.

I heard freedom bells. Walls were torn down and my eyes were opened. I could see forgiveness in a whole new light, the kind of forgiveness Christ extended to us.

"Before we even admitted wrong doing, he made a way to forgive us and extended love to us." (Romans 5:8) I had the privilege to extend love and "forgive as Christ forgives me." (Ephesians 4:32) Oh the beauty in it!

It's been said that, "Un-forgiveness is like taking poison but expecting someone else to die." Or like, "choosing to stay trapped in a jail cell of bitterness, serving time for another's crime."

"When they hurled insults at Jesus, he didn't retaliate; when he suffered, he made no threats. Instead, he entrusted himself to Him who judges justly." (1 Peter 2:23)

> We can entrust ourselves to God.
> Don't be foolish.
> Put down the poison and walk out of the jail cell.
> Forgiveness is the way, no kidding!

LET IT SNOW

Come now, and let us reason together,
says the Lord.
Though your sins are like scarlet,
they shall be white as snow;
though they are red like crimson,
they shall be like wool.

Isaiah 1 : 18

LET IT SNOW

Ever noticed that the cute white painted brick house down the street begins to look awfully dirty once the snow falls to meet its foundation? Or had a shirt with a stain on it that no product could remove? You try to fight the stain by using bleach, stain stick, special methods, and still the stain shows through? You just can't find the remedy.

Do you try to fight your "stains" apart from Christ? Striving to cover up your mess? Or maybe you don't think you're a mess at all? Maybe you're like the "painted white house" that hasn't been laid against the bright white snow just yet? The truth is, we must see ourselves as we truly are so we can see Him as He truly is! He is the snow and we are that house. We must understand that we look awfully dirty in light of God's purity.

Crimson was the dye used in biblical times, colorfast, sticking to cloth, not fading or washing away, permanent. Crimson is meant to paint a clear picture of our sin. It can't be covered up, and can't be removed in our own efforts. There is always a trace of it and there is only one remedy—

Take heart, it is snowing at the foot of the cross ... It is there that you can bring all your "stains". Come honest and confess and find Jesus there. He will wash you whiter than snow. Let His mercy and grace snow down on you!

Let it Snow, Let it Snow, Let it Snow!

NEW NICKNAME

These are the ones
I look on with favor:
those who are humble
and contrite in spirit,
and who tremble at my word.

Isaiah 66 : 2

NEW NICKNAME

Do you have a nickname?
Nicknames at our house go a mile long:
Squirrel, Bug, Mama Duck, Buddy, Wildman, Delores,
Honey Bear, Love Bug, Baby Girl.
It's sweet to be called by a nickname. It's endearing, really.
Who doesn't love it?

But what if I called you Adam for a nickname?
Would you find that bizarre?
Probably so—that doesn't sound so cute or special.

But really, we all could be nicknamed Adam at one time or
another, or Eve if you'd prefer; either would fit.

Why's that?
Because we are all quick to blame.
"It's your fault." "She made me do it." "He made me do it."

We take after Adam and Eve ...
When God asked Adam about eating from the tree He
commanded him not to, he blamed, "It was the woman."
Eve blamed, 'The serpent deceived me." (Genesis 3:12,13)

Any way you slice it, "blaming" has been around a
long time.

Have you ever pointed at someone?
When you do, there are three fingers pointing back at you.

What's your nickname?

Mine has been "Blaming" or "Eve" way too often.
I'd prefer to drop this completely. I want another nickname.

"Responsible" or "Accountable",
Or, best yet, call me "Contrite".
Now that is an endearing name.
This would reflect a broken and humble heart.
This would be refreshing; this would be God's work.

"A broken and contrite heart You, God, will not despise."
 (Psalm 51:17)

"Whoever conceals his transgressions will not prosper, but
he who confesses and forsakes them will obtain mercy."
(Proverbs 28:13)

Lord, help us all, for we are quick to blame.
Develop us into people with contrite hearts,
so we can turn toward forgiveness and prosper;
so we can find mercy and be refreshed by Your presence.
We give You all the praise.

Give us all a new nickname!

THE GAVEL MUST FALL

The man without the Spirit
does not accept the things
that come from the Spirit of God,
for they are foolishness to him,
he cannot understand
because they are spiritually discerned.

1 Corinthians 2 : 14

No eye has seen, no ear has heard,
no mind has conceived
what God has prepared for those who love Him—
but God has revealed it to us by His Spirit.

1 Corinthians 2 : 9-10

THE GAVEL MUST FALL

I was the mother of a one and a four-year-old. My Nana often came for slumber parties while my husband was away offshore fishing. I was always close to my Nana, but we grew a new bond in my adult years, priceless times that will forever hold a special place in my heart.

I can still remember the first of many long talks starting at the kitchen table one morning after breakfast. Curiosity had set in over her faith, she was full of questions. She was invested in having a heart understanding and was deeply searching and open with me.

There were more sleepovers, lunches and time to chat. I can still see her scooting to the edge of the couch, leaning in to hear the good news of the gospel.

I prayerfully considered how to assist her to see. I would speak scripture plainly, draw pictures, listen intently. I desperately wanted her to personally comprehend God's love and His plan through Jesus, to trust fully and to know her faith was secure.

It was Sunday service and the pastor's sermon referenced the gavel at a Supreme Court hearing. He was paralleling the power of the gavel to the power of the Holy Spirit. The gavel is struck against a sounding block, a striking surface to enhance its sounding qualities. It was explained that the Holy Spirit is the sounding block, enhancing and making clear the whole truth of the gospel. Without the Holy Spirit, no-one can understand. (1 Corinthians 2:9-10) I was reminded that the truth of the gospel is only spiritually discerned.

About a week later, I found myself visiting my Nana at her kitchen counter. In this sacred moment, she casually turned away from me and then back toward me. Her eyes met mine, and slowly lifting her hand she quietly asked, "Do you want this honey?"

My heart skipped a beat. In the hand of my dear Nana was a gavel. She held a gavel; my heart held great hope. The Holy Spirit held the power. The Lord held this moment and held her answers.

Maybe there is someone who you desire to know the truth, to receive Christ? Maybe that someone is you?

Let's pray the words of Ephesians 1:18 – "I pray that the eyes of their heart might be enlightened in order that they may know the hope to which You have called them, to know the riches of Your glorious inheritance."

By Your Holy Spirit Lord,
*we pray the **gavel will fall.***
Amen.

HURRY UP &
SLOW DOWN

This is the day that the Lord has made.

We will rejoice and be glad in it.

Psalm 118 : 24

HURRY UP & SLOW DOWN

It had been another full day.
We scattered in the morning, each to their own destination.
And there we were, back home again.
Where did the day go?
What precious moments did we each take away?

You know the routine.
Time to get up!
Hurry down for breakfast!
Hurry up! Time to go!
Dinner's ready! Hurry up to the table!

We had made it there, all four of us gathered for dinner.
Chatter filled the room as we shoveled in our food.

But then there was a pause ...
We all looked up.
The room became very quiet.

Our son had a heartfelt look on his face as he spoke
these words—
"Can y'all please pray for me?
Pray that I would live in the moment."

He explained that even as we sat there together, his mind was somewhere else.

He was missing the moment.
He was thinking about what he was going to do when he got up.
"I do this all the time and I just want this to change," he said.

Whoa, can't we all use that prayer?

We all bowed our heads and prayed, knowing this prayer was not just for him, but for all of us.

Too many times we miss the moment.
We rush through our days.
We are robbed by thinking about what's next.

Lord, teach us to be present and help us to not miss the moments.

Let's Hurry Up and Slow Down!

SWEET & SALTY

You are the salt of the earth.
You are the light of the world.

Matthew 5 : 13-14

Do everything without
grumbling or complaining.

Philippians 2 : 14-16

SWEET & SALTY

At our house we have a common saying,
"You're being salty!"
This indicates that someone is being rude, moody,
complaining and unapproachable.
Frankly, you don't want to be around them.
It doesn't win friends; there is absolutely nothing
sweet about it.

My family has called me out on this.
I am not innocent.
It's not just teenagers found guilty.
Unfortunately, I have been this kind of salty.

I'd much rather be described as sweet.

There's only one kind of salty I want to be ...
The kind that seasons the lives of others with love and light.

"You are the salt of the earth. But what good is salt if it has lost its flavor?" (Mathew 5:13)

"Let your speech always be with grace, as though seasoned with salt, so that you will know how you should respond to each person." (Colossians 4:6)

It's only when we are sweet that we are actually salty!

THE STONE
IS ROLLED AWAY

*Who will roll away the stone for us
from the entrance to the tomb?*

Mark 16 : 3

THE STONE
IS ROLLED AWAY

There was a heavy stone at the entry—
It seemed immovable.
The tomb was dark and cold.
It seemed the end.

Who would roll the stone away?

God would ... God did ...
He removed what seemed immovable.
He did the impossible.
The tomb filled with light.
It wasn't the end.
Jesus had risen!

There was heavy stone at the door of our hearts.
We were shut off from life now and life eternal.

We've all felt the darkness and coldness—
in our hearts and in this world.
There are times when we feel at the end.

We can try to pretend,
but our hearts long for something more.

Look up, it's Jesus, no longer on the cross,
but risen and ascended!
He lives that we might live.
Let Him roll away the stone of your doubts and fears.
Let Him bring you out of the tomb into the Light.

Trust in Jesus and rise to new life.
Never again will there be inescapable darkness.

Our hearts were made to know Him.
Our hearts were made to walk this life with Him.
We can approach the throne of grace with confidence.
(Hebrews 4:16)
He does the impossible, removes the immovable.

Give Him your heart of stone.
He will give you a new heart and put a new spirit in you.
(Ezekiel 36:26)

He is risen and reigning!
He is mighty to save.
Rise to new life.

The stone is rolled away—Hallelujah!

JUST TRY IT

Whoever is in Christ is a new creation,
the old is gone,
the new has come!

2 Corinthians 5 : 17

JUST TRY IT

Insanity is defined as doing the same thing over and over
again, expecting a different result.
Round and round you go.
It's mind blowing and tiring,
exhausting and crazy.
Uh-oh, now that I think about it, I think I could be insane!

Have you ever done this?
If you have, then you know.
If you haven't, don't try it, I must warn you!

One of my dearest loves told me recently that he doesn't
have another answer. "This is just how it is, it's just how I
am. When I get upset and angry, I don't know any
other way."

He went so far as to ask me how I choose to respond in a
different way;
made it sound like I always get it right.
Hello!!! Please, please, let me assure you that I do not.
But, it got me thinking ...

What I have discovered is this ...
You can and must often act BEFORE you feel like it.
You can choose to DO what is right, even when you don't
feel like doing it at all.

Only then do you have the opportunity to see the better way.
Try it.

This small step can't happen without a BIG helper.
It's the Lord Himself who is your big support.
Receive Him into your life and into the moment.
Ask and He will assist you.

Not sure it's true?
I challenge you to give it a shot.
You won't be disappointed, I promise.
He is in the business of making people new.

Tell Jesus how much you need Him.
Receive Him at all times, in all situations.
Step out even if you don't feel like it.

It's mind blowing.
He will take you out of the insane cycle into a glorious new way!

Try it.

RELIABLE SOURCE

For the word of God
is alive and powerful.
It is sharper than
the sharpest two-edged sword,
cutting between soul and spirit,
between joint and marrow.
It exposes
our innermost thoughts and desires.

Hebrews 4 : 12

RELIABLE SOURCE

Looking for the answer?
"Just google it" or "Ask Siri".

Who is Siri? How does she know so much anyway?

I heard the conversation from the other room.
It was my girlfriends.
There was chatter about something they learned on
the internet.
It sounded a little far-fetched but they were almost
convinced that it was true.

It got me thinking.

It's okay to search the internet to get quick information
that is direct,
but we need to exercise caution if we are searching for
life answers.

How many of us rely on the computer to spit out answers
to us for the deeper things in life?
Most anything can be punched in the browser with several
options for answers.
But what's the truth?
Because, honestly, we can pick the answer our
"itching ears" want to hear. (2 Timothy 4:3)
This can be dangerous.

Did you know that there's a reliable place to go and always get the right answer beyond a shadow of a doubt?

It's God's Holy Word.
It's the only reliable source.
"For ALL Scripture is GOD-breathed. It is useful for teaching, rebuking, correcting and training in righteousness."
(2 Timothy 3:16)

How does the Bible know so much anyway?
God is the author.
His Word is irrefutable.
It's the raw truth, the whole story.
All other "searches" will prove tainted.

"The Bible is the one book to which any thoughtful man may go with any honest question of life or destiny and find the answer of God by honest searching." (Billy Graham)

The Google bar is good for a few small things,
but, when it comes to the bigger things in life,
stop searching the internet and instead search His Word.

It's the whole truth and nothing but the truth.

Check it out!

THREE WOODEN CROSSES

*I tell you the truth,
today you will be with me in paradise.*

Luke 23 : 43

THREE WOODEN CROSSES

I was making a road trip to visit my relative on the farm.
It was a clear sunny day in the early summer.
I left behind the city and came to open, rolling hills.

I gazed up on the hill.
Against the backdrop of the infinite clear blue sky,
there stood three wooden crosses.
Not one, but three.

All three, making the message as clear as the sky.

Jesus hung in the middle,
Two criminals on either side.
The innocent One surrounded by the guilty ones.

One beside Jesus mocking Him and hurling insults at Him.
The other begging for Jesus's mercy.
(Luke 23:39, 42)

One rejected Jesus. The other received Jesus.

Isn't that us?

Jesus, the innocent One, in the middle of our guilty mess.
Each of us with a choice.

Just as the criminals decided in their own hearts how they would respond to Jesus, so too must we.

Jesus awaits our response. He is trustworthy.
Don't wait until the end to receive Him.

Have you made a choice?

Secure your today and your tomorrow.
There are three wooden crosses.
Choose the "One" in the middle.
He is dying to reach you.
Receive His grace and mercy.
Paradise awaits.

"For the grace of God has appeared that offers salvation to all people." (Titus 2:11)

Lord, you don't tell us to clean up our mess and then come to You. We thank you that your amazing grace comes to save us right in the middle of our mess! Amen.

RIGHT-HAND MAN

So do not fear, for I am with you,

do not be dismayed,

for I am your God

I will strengthen you and help you

I will uphold you

with my righteous right hand.

Isaiah 41 : 10

RIGHT-HAND MAN

I have always loved this verse.
It's probably because
I am prone to fear and dismay.
I often stumble and feel weak.
This verse reminds me
to lean on "my right-hand man".

A right-hand man is defined as an
indispensable helper.

Indispensable implies imperative, crucial, of
utmost importance, vital, must-have, essential
and invaluable.

I know I can count on my dear husband and
extended family. I have friends that will be my
friends until the end, but, they can't uphold
me the way that the Lord can.

People are flawed.
They will ultimately disappoint.
Their love is wavering and incomplete.
Eventually, their strength runs out.
They get tired of holding you.

There is really only one right-hand man
you can truly count on.

He will never disappoint.
He will be there into eternity.
He will uphold you.

His right hand denotes authority,
blessing, sovereignty, and strength.

We can trust His grasp!

SHORT ON WORDS

In the same way the Spirit
also helps our weakness;
for we do not know how to pray
as we should,
but the Spirit himself
intercedes for us
with groanings too deep for words;
He who searches the hearts
knows what the mind of the Spirit is, because He
intercedes for the saints according to the will of God.

Romans 8 : 26-27

SHORT ON WORDS

By end of most days,
I'm ready to throw my cell phone in the trash.
I never land on the right keys to form the words I intend.
I can't even get my thumbs to work the keyboard.
I use my index finger (a dead give-away to my age).
Words show up on my screen that I never knew existed.
Then there's voice text—Siri always hears me wrong.
It wears me out!

Forget the phone, how about in person?
I always come up short on words.
I often have a hard time trying to explain myself.

Ever had a long day?
You just wanted to have someone listen and understand?
Or a mountaintop experience you wanted to share?
Or you were hurting and needed an ear and a shoulder?
You try, but you fail to express yourself.

Others just don't get you.
You can't utter the right words,
let alone express your deepest feelings.
You never say it quite right.
It all comes up short.

Good news!

There is someone we can talk to.
He gets the heart of the matter.
When we are short on words,
He knows how to fill in the blanks.
He always hears us right.
He can read between the lines and put a voice to it all.

Our "groanings too deep for words" do not go unheard.
The Holy Spirit searches us and knows how to say it
just right.
He takes it all to the throne of grace.
He beautifully intercedes on our behalf.
And He does it all in line with God's perfect will.

It's okay if we are short on words.
He helps us in our weakness.

Put down the cell phone.
No texting needed. No lengthy drawn out words necessary.
Just a weak heart with a dull whisper will do ... "I need You".

Short on words?
Just go to Him. He will fill in the blanks.
He never comes up short.

RECKLESS

*God demonstrates
His own love for us in this:
while we were still sinners,
Christ died for us.*

Romans 5 : 8

RECKLESS

I opened my Bible and out fell my traffic violation receipt. How had it ended up in there? I was charged that day for speeding and deserved reckless, but the officer kindly reported my speed lower. My official court receipt reflected my final charge as "defective equipment". It read **Paid in Full** and, just underneath, my name was clearly marked.

The day I stood before the judge, I quickly pleaded guilty but begged a break and was amazed with this final outcome.

What in the world?

There's another charge against me and I deserve reckless.
The judge was right that day.
I do have "defective equipment"
— it's my heart.
I am guilty.
In fact, we are all guilty.

I opened my Bible and these words fell out. "We all have sinned and fallen short of God's glorious standard." And, you see, "at just the right time, when we were still powerless, Christ died for the ungodly. Very rarely will anyone die for a righteous person, though for a good person someone might possibly dare to die. But God demonstrates His own love for us in this: While we were still sinners, Christ died for us." (Romans 5:6-8)

Did you hear that? I mean, we didn't even beg a break and He stepped in and covered our penalty. He lifted the whole charge. It was Paid in Full by the blood of Christ, the only acceptable payment. (Romans 5:9)

Christ served the sentence we deserved.

What in the world?

> God is just AND God is love.
> By grace we've been saved—
> and this is not from ourselves,
> it is the gift of God.
> (Ephesians 2:8)

Plead guilty and be amazed with this final outcome!

Reckless heart, reckless love!

RAIN & RAINBOWS

The rain came down,
the streams rose,
and the winds blew against the house,
yet it did not fall,
because its foundation
was on the rock.

Matthew 7 : 25

RAIN & RAINBOWS

I was immersed in the salty ocean water.
The fresh rain poured down on me.
I stood in awe as I witnessed the colors on the horizon.
A rainbow arched full and bright.
It touched down on both sides.
Then another full rainbow appeared above it.

Vibrant, bright, beautiful—
Screaming His nearness and His promises.

Only with the sunshine AND the rain is a rainbow possible.

Oh, how this spoke to me and calmed my soul.

Lord, You are beautiful in every way.
You are chasing me in the rain,
in my clouds these days.
Right now, You paint the sky.
You are near.

I settled back into my beach chair and opened my email.
What is this?

A friend I rarely hear from had emailed to say
she'd been praying for me.

Lord, thank You that when I feel defeated
and can hardly utter any real words in prayer,
You keep pursuing me with Your love
and prick the hearts of others to lift me up.
You have me covered.
You lift me, in the clouds, in the rain.
In the stillness I am reminded,
"You keep your promises always, not because I am
faithful, but because You are."
(2 Timothy 2:13)

I exited the restaurant late that evening for the encore,
only this time the backdrop was the dark night sky.
A bright star danced and shot across the expanse.
It quickly faded to nothing.

In the rain and rainbows He showers me with His presence!

Let your soul be still and rest.
He is near.
He is showering you too!

UNTO HIM

Work willingly, with all your heart,
at whatever you do,
as though you were working
for the Lord
rather than for people.

Do your best.
Work from the heart
for your real Master,
for God.

Colossians 3 : 23

UNTO HIM

It was a regular day driving around Richmond.
I was busy daydreaming in the car as usual.
I often have a hard time keeping up with
my speeding thoughts.
They race from one thing to another.

I looked up and my mind hit the brake.
It was the license plate on the car passing in front of me.
"Unto Him," it announced.

My racing thoughts took the first exit and I found myself
fixed on just these two words, "Unto Him."
I then thought, "NOT Unto me."

Are you looking for applause and not getting it?
Disappointed because nobody is noticing the good things
you are doing?
Have you hoped for a thank you and they are few and
far between?
Does it seem that nobody is acknowledging your efforts?

You are not alone.
I have been there.

There's a deeper truth to be fixed on,
a better road to take.
"Unto Him" implies a whole new way.
Exiting from self proves a better drive every time.
He deserves all the honor and praise.

"Truly I tell you, whatever you did for one of the least
of these brothers and sisters of mine, you did for me."
(Matthew 25:40)

Unto You Lord, Unto You

I have heard it said, and need to hear it again,
Live for the audience of One.

Lord, help me, help us, to live for You and You alone.
Keeping You in view,
Our Savior, Provider & Sustainer.

It's really all about You!

ROCK SOLID

Anyone who listens to my teaching
and follows it
is wise,
like a person who builds a house
on solid rock.

Matthew 7:24

ROCK SOLID

It was early this morning, I noticed all the debris—
moss, leaves, grass clippings, pollen,
all in a meaningless pile on our back stoop—
a mess really, useless, just lying there.

I glanced up and noticed a little bird's nest in the making.

I returned home only a few hours later.
The pile that once laid strewn about was gone.
The birds hadn't wasted any time, they had taken action.
The debris was gone and now beautifully woven together.
I stared up at the amazing work,
each piece had its purpose.
The nest sat nestled under the shelter of our carport.
In the end, they had built a sturdy place to live,
right beside our outdoor light.

But this is strictly "for the birds".

"For the birds" insinuates trivial and worthless,
but these birds had done nothing trivial.
It was of great worth to them, a safe place to live.

These birds are onto something,
for we must build our lives as they do.

We must take action.
Invest our time.
Gather up all the meaningful pieces of His Word.
Trust them and weave them into our hearts.
Apply them and see that every piece has its purpose.

"Every word proves true." (Proverbs 30:5)
We will be amazed at the work He will do.

In the end, this builds a safe, "solid rock" place to live …
In His truth and in His light.

"I trust in Your Word." (Psalm 119:42)

Get to building …
This is of great worth …
This isn't for the birds!

WELCOME HOME PARTY

But while he was still a long way off,
his father saw him
and was filled
with compassion for him,
he ran to his son,
threw his arms around him
and kissed him.

Luke 15 : 20

WELCOME HOME PARTY

I grabbed my floral hard-sided suitcase and collected handfuls of random clothes and stuffed animals. I was only nine years old, but I was running away. It was after supper, just before dark. I was in my pajamas as I stomped to the front door and turned to go. Our sidewalk stretched about 100 steps. I made every effort to not look back as I walked away, but deep down I wondered if they were watching me. I stood at the street curb for what seemed like forever, secretly wanting them to beg me back. In no time I was bolting back to the front door and into their arms. I realized that I'd never want to leave the ones that love me most.

I didn't make it far that day, but there's another that I know who did. In fact, he left for a long while, taking his inheritance and squandering it on wild living. He left and didn't look back, he didn't call home, let alone think of the one who loved him most. But, that all changed when it all came up empty. The money was gone and he had nothing and nobody. The one thing he did have was a broken heart with deep regret. So he came home empty handed with a heartfelt apology.

"When his father saw him off in the distance, he was filled with compassion, ran to him, threw his arms around him and kissed him."

The son said, "I have sinned against heaven and against you. I am no longer worthy to be called your son." (Luke 15:20-21)

And guess what?

The party began!

His Dad called for a fattened calf, ring for his finger and sandals for his feet. "My son was lost and now he is found!" (Luke 15:24)

I was never lost that day. My parents kept a close eye on me, waiting for me to turn around. Jesus keeps a close eye too and He longs for us to turn to Him and come home.

To squander is to waste something in a reckless and foolish manner. To allow an opportunity to be lost. Jesus has an eternal inheritance He offers that should not be squandered.

"What good is it for someone to gain the whole world, yet forfeit their soul?" (Mark 8:36)

Let's not squander this extravagant, costly gift.
Let's not leave the One who loves us most.
It's no secret, He deeply wants us home,
now and forevermore.

Can you see Him off in the distance?
He is moved with compassion.

DO THE MATH

Enter His gates with thanksgiving
and His courts with praise;
give thanks to Him
and praise His name.

Psalm 100 : 4

DO THE MATH

Do you like math?

I have a dear lifelong friend who's been teaching it for years. She does an amazing job instructing middle school girls. Algebra is her expertise.

Do you remember that course?
Always solving the answer for the unknown.

It occurred to me recently,
Life can be like an equation, too.

When we are down and want to get up ...
Thankfulness is the answer.
X = Be thankful.

Take a close look at your equation.
Does it include griping and grumbling?
This doesn't add up to much more than misery.
I've tried it!
This = zero.

Low on thanksgiving?
Go to Ephesians 1:3-14 and begin to count.
Count all we have to be thankful for.
We are blessed with every spiritual blessing in Christ.

Adopted + redeemed + forgiven + lavished with grace + chosen + included in Christ + marked with His Holy Spirit + lavished with wisdom and understanding + have a guaranteed inheritance = overwhelming reasons to be thankful

Been whining and bickering?
Feel up against a wall?
Distanced from the ones you love and from the Lord?

The answer to overcoming isn't unknown.
The Lord does an amazing job instructing us.
We know how to solve this.

"Enter His gates with thanksgiving and His courts with praise." (Psalm 100:4)

Do the math—this adds up!

*Lord, help us to subtract complaining and arguing from our lives. To practice adding in thankfulness and praise that brings us into Your courts and trumps it all. We love and thank You for all the spiritual blessings that are ours in You! We are so glad that You always have the answer key.
Amen.*

DANDELIONS

Pray without ceasing.

1 Thessalonians 5 : 17

DANDELIONS

I leaned over, picked one up and blew
    as hard as I could.
I watched the feathery shoots float away,
    carried by the wind.

Chances are, you've wished on a dandelion before.
You know this common weed
    that shoots up wherever it lands.
It looks like a fuzzy ball,
    with umbrella-like extensions.
With a faint breeze or a faint breath,
    the extensions disperse into the air.
Up, up and away they go.
They are carried sometimes miles away.
Who knows where they will all land?

Wishing on a dandelion is one thing.
Praying to the One
      who is in charge of the wind is another.

"The wind blows wherever it pleases. You hear its sound,
but you cannot tell where it comes from or where it is
going. So it is with The Spirit." (John 3:8)

And so it is with our prayers.

He takes them and carries them in for a safe landing.
Secured in His power and His will.

GO THE DISTANCE

Do you not know that in a race
all the runners run,
but only one gets the prize?
Run in such a way as to get the prize.
Everyone who competes in the games
goes into strict training.
They do it to get a crown
that will not last,
but we do it to get a crown
that will last forever.

1 Corinthians 9 : 24-25

GO THE DISTANCE

It was summer and I laced up my shoes for a run.
I was invited to tag along with my daughter and boyfriend.
The heat was on, I'd show them this ole girl could keep up.

With my eyes up and my breathing steady,
I had a great rhythm to my race.
Not once did I stop, I was amazed how light I felt
on my feet.
The training I had been consistently doing had paid off.

We didn't run a marathon distance,
but it was an impressive feat.
Surprisingly, I could have probably pushed
and gone further.
I was in it to win it and cross the finish line.

Yesterday I found myself lagging behind in a
different race—

The daily run of life itself.
I didn't desire to lace up my shoes, let alone put them on.
I had nothing steady going on.
My eyes had dropped, my heart too.
There was no rhythm to my race; I was too tired to try.
My feet were heavy and I could barely push through
the day.
All I could do was to put one foot in front of the other.
I wanted to turn in my shoes and drop out of the race.

We know that training is necessary and it pays off in a physical race.
How much more in faith?
We are not in a quick sprint, but a lifelong marathon.

I'm finding that the key to going the distance is where I place my gaze.

In the words of a Vacation Bible School favorite ...
Run the race, keep the pace, and keep your eyes on Jesus.

Only then can this ole girl keep the pace,
Only then will any of us stay in the race.

Feeling tired?
Let's Remember WHO we are running for ...

"Let us run with perseverance the race marked out for us, fixing our eyes on Jesus, the Author and Perfecter of faith." (Hebrews 12:1-2)

> Run for Him.
> Keep going, steady pace, eyes up.
> Lace up your shoes. The heat is on.
> Jesus is for us.
> He will help us go the distance.
> He will help us cross the finish line.

Jesus, we long to run, for You and to You.
We praise You!

HIS ULTIMATE PLAN

For I know the plans I have for you,
declares the Lord,
plans to prosper you
and not to harm you,
plans to give you hope and a future.

Jeremiah 29 : 11

HIS ULTIMATE PLAN

It was back during our kids' middle school years.
It was an uneasy time growing up.
It happened one night at bedtime.
I began praying the above verse aloud with our kids.

Thereafter, it ended up becoming a constant reminder.
Any time of the day,
we would say it to each other regularly and pray it often.
We all still do.
We've tagged Jeremiah 29:11 as our family verse
for years now.

It is comforting to remind ourselves,
that the Lord declares His plans are good,
with hope and a future.

But what if we keep reading?
He has so much more to say.

"Then you will call on Me and come and pray to Me, and I
will listen to you. You will seek Me and find Me when you
seek Me with all your heart. I will be found by you."
(Jeremiah 29:12-14)

Do you hear that?
His ultimate plan—
That we search and know Him,
The One who holds our present and secures our future.
This is really where we prosper.
This is where we find living hope.

Life is full of uneasy times.
Call and pray to Him. Seek and find Him.
"He would not tell us to seek Him if He couldn't be found."
(Isaiah 45:19)

He is listening.

This is His best plan for our lives!
All other plans pale in comparison.

GROUP EXERCISE

And let us consider how
we may spur one another on
toward love and good deeds,
not giving up meeting together,
as some are in the habit of doing,
but encouraging one another—
and all the more
as you see the Day approaching.

Hebrews 10 : 24-25

GROUP EXERCISE

There I was at the gym, in a boot camp class.
I was pushing hard, trying not to watch the clock.
Just one more jumping jack, one more burpee,
    one more push up.
Sweat beading up on my forehead. Wiping my brow.

It's become a habit to go to the gym and I love it.
It is beneficial to my whole day. I can't afford to miss.
I am a regular.

I am a big fan of group exercise.
If I had to get myself exercising without everyone else,
    you can forget it.
I would probably lose interest and not stay the course.

I jog past a friend and they call out, "Go, Go, Go!"
I pass someone else and yell out to them the same.
The encouragement helps me to push.
We spur each other on, there is nothing like it.
We all manage to press on to the end.

Likewise, we are called to persevere in faith.
Guess what the key is?
You got it ... Group Exercise!

Meeting together is paramount.

We need each other to stay in shape.
We need each other so that we don't give up,
    to call each other out when we are slipping in faith,
    to push each other toward one more act of love,
    to assure one another that God is in control,
    to remind each other of His love and promises,
    to cheer each other on in life,
    to open His Holy Word together,
    and to press on to the end.

Going to the gym is a great habit.
Creating the habit of gathering
    with others in faith is even better.
It is crucial in our lives, we can't afford to miss.

Are you a regular at group exercise?

Lord, thank You that You gave us each other to lean on and walk through life with. Help us to consider the importance of cheering each other and intentionally being a part of a group so we can be strengthened and strengthen others in faith. Amen.

UNEXPECTED GIFT

Why do you look at the speck of sawdust
in your brother's eye and pay no attention
to the plank in your own eye?

Luke 6 : 41

UNEXPECTED GIFT

"I now pronounce you man and wife."
We sealed it with a kiss at the altar;
walked hand in hand down the aisle
as husband and wife.
The reception proved perfect.
Our honeymoon week came and went.
We headed home to face the rest of our lives together.
Who knew what we'd see in our future?

We got so many amazing wedding gifts,
one in particular that I hadn't quite expected.

It was a friend who helped me uncover the value
of this gift.

Let me explain—I have to be honest.
I was struggling as a new wife,
trying to navigate this new territory.
It was a hard adjustment not being all about me.
I was quickly on a mission to fix my husband.

In my struggle I would continually point out his flaws.
It was then I had a wake-up call.

It was then I gained insight about this gift I had been given.

It came when a friend asked me,
"Why do you refuse to look at your own heart?"

What was the gift?
A full length mirror.
Not literally, but figuratively.

I definitely hadn't hung it up.
I hadn't even looked at myself, no not once.

Jesus said: "Why do you look at the speck of sawdust in
your brother's eye and pay no attention to the plank in your
own eye?" (Luke 6:41)

We are all prone to pointing the finger, married or not.
I really needed to look at my own heart, we all do.

Jesus will show us our planks.
He will remake us and renew our relationships.

Congratulations!
You have been gifted with a full length mirror, too.
This gift may be unexpected,
but once used, it proves to be the best gift of all.
It's the gift that keeps on giving.

Take a look, you'll like what you see in your future!

IN THE WAITING

Even youths shall faint and be weary
and young men stumble and fall,
but they who wait for the Lord
shall renew their strength;
they shall mount up with wings like eagles;
they shall run and not be weary,
they shall walk and not faint.

Isaiah 40 : 30-31

IN THE WAITING

Did you hear that?
Those who "wait" on the Lord shall renew their strength.
So, it's in the waiting that we become strong then?
But, it's so hard to wait and I often feel so weak
in the waiting.
Let's think on this one.

We'd all agree that waiting seems to be a
big part of what we do.
In the everyday, we wait in line, wait for a green light,
for a returned phone call or text, for pay day,
the weekend or vacation.

This kind of waiting is like a walk in the park.
The kind that involves heart-wrenching circumstances,
broken relationships, trials and uncertainty—
now that's a tough wait—
far harder than waiting on the green.

If we are honest, we easily stumble and fall into weariness
in the waiting.

What about a different kind?

"In the morning, Lord, you hear my voice; in the morning
I lay my requests before you and wait expectantly."
(Psalm 5:3)

To be expectant is to look for something actively, intently
and with longing. It is to strongly believe that something is
going to happen, or someone is likely to do something.

How many times do I take off my wings and become
faint and hopeless?
How many times do I lay my requests before Him and
forget to anticipate and look for Him?

I'm taken by His reminder to expect Him to respond.
I'm reminded that it will be in His way and in His time.

Yes, waiting seems part of His purpose whether we like it
or not, and sometimes He has to tell us more than once—

Wait for the Lord; be strong and take heart and
wait for the Lord. (Psalm 27:14)

Let's take heart, take courage.
He is near.
Waiting expectantly is how we put on our wings.

*Lord, Your presence strengthens us in the waiting. We
can expect You. Keep our eyes open and actively looking.
There is no place you are not. In all our waiting, thank you
that you are there to lift us. You never grow tired or weary.
(Isaiah 40:28) Amen.*

RETURNS

Even now, declares the Lord,
return to me with all your heart,
with fasting and weeping
and mourning.
Rend your heart
and not your garments.
Return to the Lord your God,
for He is gracious and compassionate,
slow to anger and abounding in love.

Joel 2 : 12-13

RETURNS

Returns ...
You know the routine.
Stand in line, wait your turn.
Do you have a receipt?
What card did you put it on?
Will you get cash back or a store credit?

We have all made returns before.
When you make a return, it is the act of returning the item
back to the place it belongs.

What about a different kind of return?

We are all invited ...
"Return to me with all your heart, even now, rend your
heart," declares the Lord.

To "rend" was a custom back in the day.
It involved someone vigorously tearing their clothing as a
visible sign of deep emotion.
It was an outward way of showing inward feelings.

We make our return by rendering not our garments,
but our hearts.

Broken, split apart and torn, with deep genuine sorrow.
It can't be mustered up.
It's a gift from God.

In His grace, He breaks our hearts for what breaks His.

"For godly sorrow brings repentance that leads to salvation and leaves no regret, but worldly sorrow brings death." (2 Corinthians 7:10)

"It produces an eagerness to clear yourself, with longing and readiness." (2 Corinthians 7:11)

Return ...
There's no line to stand in, no wait.
Bring your whole broken heart.
Jesus will meet and greet you with love
and grace un-ending.
He will pour out compassion on you.
Return to where you belong.
His arms are open.

This is the best kind of return to make!

A GOOD LOOK

You were taught, with regard to your former way
of life, to put off your old self to be made new
in the attitude of your minds; and put on
the new self, created to be like God
in true righteousness and holiness.

Ephesians 4 : 22-24

A GOOD LOOK

I finished my class at the gym, gathered in the hall and was talking to friends. I glanced down and I laughed to myself. I had left the house with two different shoes on! One old and one new. Not a good look!

How often do I do this? Maybe not two different shoes, but mixed devotion. Not my shoes, but my attitude, my outlook, my old ways, my old habits. I often grab them from my closet. Not a good look!

I have this bad habit of gathering my old things to donate to the Goodwill but then hold onto them and drive around town with my donations in the back of my car, forgetting to drop them off.

Did you know we can drop off our old ways to Christ? In exchange, He will give us new ways.

We must have this habit of gathering our "donations" for Jesus and dropping them off. He willingly receives them ... old habits, old ways, misdirected thoughts, weariness, bitterness, you name it! It's the great exchange!

He gives back two new shoes to walk out a new life in Him.

This is a good look!

SEARCH ENGINE

Call to me,
ask me, and I will answer you,
and will tell you
unsearchable, great and hidden things,
remarkable secrets
you have not known.

Jeremiah 33 : 3

SEARCH ENGINE

I couldn't get a signal.
I kept going back to the search bar on my computer ...
nothing.
It wouldn't even load.
So frustrating.
Can't I just search?

I was seeking to uncover important insights.
I was on a mission to get some answers to future planning.
I was trying all sorts of searches, all different angels.
Maybe this time I would type in the correct phrase.
Maybe this time it would be revealed.
But, no, the signal wouldn't even work.
No searching available.

There I was in the quiet ...
I quickly realized that this was no coincidence,
for I was searching in the wrong place.

I bowed my head and instead called out in prayer.
I can always get a strong signal here.
No fancy angle or phrase necessary.
I cry out any words and the search is clear.

"He searches every heart and understands every desire and thought." (1 Chronicles 28:9)

Call to Him and He will tell you unsearchable things.
Ask Him, He is the One who holds the future and the secrets.
He reveals things we can never uncover apart from Him.
His insight is flawless, His wisdom beyond measure.

"Great is the Lord and most worthy of praise; His greatness no one can fathom." (Psalm 145:3)

We can always get a signal.
We can always search.
He will always answer.

Lord, help us to always search in the right place. We praise You that You share Your deepest secrets with us when we do. Amen.

HIS SHADE

The Lord watches over you—
The Lord is your shade
at your right hand.

Psalm 121:5

HIS SHADE

It was certainly not the desert,
but it was super-hot that day sitting on the dock.
Sweat beads rolled off my brow as I sat baking in the sun.
I was covered in sunscreen to stay protected.

I had traveled to the river house by myself for the weekend.
Only one beach chair sat on the dock, yet I was not alone.

I scooted over to be under the umbrella.
I felt the coolness of the breeze.
I was refreshed in the shade.

As I sat here, I remembered Jesus in the desert.
I started to recall desert places in my own life.
You know these places, we all find ourselves in them;
the places that seem parched,
the places where doubts and challenges overtake you.

I was following Jesus's lead as I sat there,
over and over again remembering;
remembering the things that are written in His Holy Word.
For when He was in the desert,
He triumphed over all lies with the truth,
repeatedly saying "For it is written".

"I have hidden His Word in my heart." (Psalm 119:11)

His Word showed forth its living power in that moment.
It was there that "He reminded me of all that He has taught
me." (John 14:26)

Under the umbrella's shade, I suddenly recalled.
Psalm 121:5-8.

"I watch over you—I am the shade at your right hand;
the sun will not harm you by day, nor the moon by night.
I will keep you from all harm—I will watch over your life;
I will watch over your coming and going
both now and forevermore."

My doubts began to melt and my challenges shrunk.
I no longer felt parched.

"After Jesus rebuked the devil in the desert with the truth,
the devil left Him, angels came to attend Him."
(Matthew 4:11)

Felt like angels were attending me too ...

I needed to reapply sunscreen to stay out on the dock. In the
same way, we need to know His truth and keep applying His
truth in all circumstances. His truth combats all lies, we will
stay protected.

Have you applied it?
Know what is written ... Rest in His shade!

TURN

Now God commands
all men everywhere
to repent.

Acts 17 : 30

TURN

I remember it well—
I was with my class of elementary age kids at a Bible study.
The lesson was on repentance.
I have always felt that a hands-on experience solidifies
the lesson.
It was no different this day.

They each stood anywhere in the room.
They would walk forward.
I would consistently call out loud, "repent".
When I did, each would do an about-face,
changing direction.

We repeated this over and over,
much like we are urged to do in real life.

We should respond to the very word that began
Jesus's ministry—

"REPENT ... For the kingdom of heaven has come near."
(Matthew 3:2)

Repentance means to turn from our sin.

Trusting in Jesus is where faith begins.
Repentance is where faith grows.

This isn't a game.

This is His loving invitation.

Will we take Him up on it?

Times of refreshing will then come from the presence of the Lord. (Acts 3:19)

"There will be more rejoicing in heaven over one sinner who repents than over ninety-nine righteous persons who do not need to repent." (Luke 15:7)

Let's respond ...
Do an about-face.
Turn toward our loving Savior.
Repeat ... over and over.
There will be much joy in heaven and much joy
in our hearts!

In Your grace, teach us to keep turning. We praise You for Your invitation to be set free. Amen.

TWO LEFT FEET

To Him who is able to keep you from stumbling
and to present you before His glorious presence
without fault and with great joy—to the only God
our Savior be glory, majesty, power and authority,
through Jesus Christ our Lord, before all ages,
now and forevermore! Amen.

Jude 1:24-25

TWO LEFT FEET

The incoming call was from my daughter.
I was away on a trip and she was inquiring if I had packed
and taken my boots like hers.
I was quick to tell her that I had them.
She was quick to tell me that I had packed
two right shoes.
The outcome was that she had two left feet.

And I thought to myself, I often do too ...

This saying, "two left feet", is often used to refer to one's
inability to dance.
The image is of a clumsy person,
unbalanced and stumbling.

My mind drifts to the all too familiar dance
with my husband.
I can feel his firm hand in mine and his strong arm
"trying" to lead.
As I resist him, the dance becomes awkward and unstable.
He looks me in the eye, "Am I leading or are you?"

Life is like a dance.

It begs the question,
Am I trusting His firm hand in mine?

"Since we live by the Spirit,
let us keep in step with the Spirit."
(Galatians 5:25)

He looks me in the eye.
He looks you in the eye.
"Will you let Me lead?"

His strong arm is more than able to lead life's dance.
He will keep us from stumbling and keep us steady.
He dances us into His glorious presence.
He is overjoyed when we trust Him to do it.

Dance, dance, dance, both now and forevermore,
through Jesus Christ our Savior. Amen.

Without Him leading we have two left feet!

DIG & PLANT

Therefore, get rid of all moral filth
and the evil that is so prevalent
and humbly accept the word
planted in you,
which can save you.

James 1:21

DIG & PLANT

It was that time of year:
Colorful flowers were popping up all around us.
Naked branches were filling out with greenery.
Pollen was falling, assisting everything to grow.
The plants were waking up.

When we moved into our home a few years back, we had
this nice surprise. The people who lived here prior to us had
planted bulbs. They spring up in abundance. We just weed
and water. They continue to grow.
We enjoy.

They did the work, we reap the benefit.

There's another kind of planting,
But we each must do the work.
We have to do the digging.

We must continually dig into God's Word.
Pride must fall so His truth can take root.
Humility must be spread to assist our response
to His Word.
Weeding is most important so to not choke
our growth.

When we do this work, we will reap the benefits.

Get to digging and planting.
Life will spring up!

WHO'S AT THE DOOR?

Sin is crouching at your door;
it desires to have you,
but you must rule over it.

Genesis 4 : 7

WHO'S AT THE DOOR?

Are you quick to open the door when you hear a knock? Or do you first see who it is before opening the door? Friends that are expected arrive to our backdoor, but when someone is at the front door, I can never be quite sure.

I have an unwanted visitor that keeps arriving in the middle of the night. I awake suddenly to what I think is someone right outside our bedroom door. I can almost see him through the crack and I'm certain he's coming in to hurt me. I grab my husband in panic and fear and wake him to help me. It is a little crazy, I know, but in the moment it seems so real.

Have you ever heard it said in scripture, that "sin is crouching at your door"?

Crouching is defined as a low bent position to avoid being seen. Well, there is certainly no one at our bedroom door, but we can be quite sure that someone is crouching at the door of our hearts and minds and he wants to hurt us.

We need to expect him. He's smooth at shaking up our thoughts and pushing our buttons to push us to despair and shame. He's slick, feeding us lies, causing discord and strife and steering us to sin. He comes to steal, kill and destroy. (John 10:10) He desires to rob our hope and silence the truth, kill our peace and keep us from life at its fullest. He wants to avoid being seen, but let's not avoid the truth. This is for real, this isn't crazy!

Invite Jesus inside.
Grab Him tight.
Don't let go.
Cling to His truth.

There's someone crouching at the door of our hearts and minds.
There's someone stronger to help and protect us.
Let Him answer the door and send the unwanted visitor away.

SOVEREIGN ANSWERS

Don't be anxious about anything,
but in every situation, by prayer and petition,
with thanksgiving,
present your requests to God.
And the peace of God
which transcends all understanding,
will guard your heart and mind
in Christ Jesus.

Philippians 4 : 6-7

The Lord is near to all who call on Him, to all
who call on Him in truth.

Psalm 145 : 18

SOVEREIGN ANSWERS

I can still remember walking into the admissions office.
It was a sweet and welcoming place
we wanted for our kids.
We proceeded to apply to the school.

As we walked through this process,
I was strong in prayer.
I had a peace beyond measure.
Without question, I knew the Lord was near.
I was so certain that this door was about to open.

But, guess what?
The door closed.

I learned through this experience.
When the Lord is near, it doesn't mean
His answer will be yes.
It means that He is near and I can trust Him.

I knew beyond a shadow of a doubt He had closed this
door. I could rest in His answer.

It's true.
"What He opens no one can shut, and what
He shuts no one can open."
(Revelation 3:7)

It's true.
He may or may not open the door we think,
but when we ask, He will always answer within His will.

His ways and His thoughts are higher than ours.
(Isaiah 55:8-9)

*Lord, may we entrust ourselves to You fully
and rest in Your sovereignty, never failing to thank You
and praise You. Knowing You are near gives us peace
beyond measure. May we rest in Your answers. Amen.*

"Your kingdom come, Your will be done." (Matthew 6:10)

HOME
SWEET HOME

Whoever dwells in the shelter of the Most High
will rest in the shadow
of the Almighty.

Psalm 91:1

HOME
SWEET HOME

"I'm home!" I yelled out as I opened the door. I had been gone four days. I expected a homecoming with lots of hugs as I opened the door, but it turned out a little less than I imagined. I found them settled on the couch, watching a favorite TV show. It's sweet to see them together, resting in the comfort of our home.

I don't say this out of a place of being upset about my welcome, but I am learning through every day events a deeper truth.

I, too, like to watch a good show, lay on the couch and escape, and there is nothing wrong with that. It is good to be home, good to kick my feet up on the couch and even better to be with my family.

BUT, what's best?

"I'm home!" I yelled out in prayer as I opened His Word. It had been days. I was embraced as I opened the pages. It turned out to be more than I ever could have imagined. I found myself settled down in my soul and I watched my heart sing. It is so sweet to be with my Savior, resting in His presence and promises.

Has your soul been settled down by the Savior?

It is sweet to dwell "in the shelter of the Most High".
To rest "in the shadow of the Almighty".

We can make our dwelling here.
It is here that we are always welcomed.
This is Home Sweet Home.

HOSANNA

Hosanna!
Blessed is He
who comes
in the name of the Lord!

John 12 : 13

HOSANNA

I awake, ready to face the day and give all I have to love Jesus. My phone is filled with a message from a friend reminding me that Jesus has overcome the world! The sun is shining. I am His and He is mine!

It's Palm Sunday. I am captured by the word "Hosanna" and picture all that were gathered there that day shouting praises and waving their palm branches at Jesus saying, "Blessed is He who comes in the name of the Lord!" I pause and see myself there, joining them in praise, expressing deep adoration and joy, in awe of Jesus. I am filled to overflowing.

But then my mind fast forwards to only days later. These same people are no longer shouting praises, but instead turning away from Jesus, denying Jesus, going with the crowd, forgetting, yelling "Crucify Him!"

I am frozen in the tracks of my mind.

What about me? What about you?

I'm reminded of how quickly I can go from praising Him to forgetting Him. From complete devotion to complete self-absorption. It sometimes doesn't take days, but only minutes or seconds.

I find myself at the foot of the cross. I look up at Jesus, suffering for this very part of me; for all my weaknesses, for my wavering love, all of my broken pieces. I keep looking up. I fix my eyes on Jesus. I take it in. He is there on my behalf. He loves me this much.

> Meet me at the foot of the cross.
> Look up. He loves you this much too.
>
> "Hosanna in the Highest!"
> "Blessed is He who comes in the name of The Lord."

LIGHTER LOAD

Come to Me, all you who are weary and burdened,
and I will give you rest.
Take My yoke upon you and learn from Me,
for I am gentle and humble in heart,
and you will find rest for your souls.
For My yoke is easy and My burden is light.

Matthew 11:28-30

LIGHTER LOAD

It's snowing again.
I notice all the paths shoveled out and
footprints can be seen everywhere.
As I peer out the window, my heart travels to a tender place
as this story unfolds—

It's me. I'm trudging in the wintery fluff,
carrying quite a load and barely keeping up.

It's Christ keeping pace up ahead of me on the snowy path.
I am weighed down, huffing and puffing.
He keeps turning around,
asking me if He can carry my load.
I politely answer, "No, I got this,"
and continue to struggle and fight.

A bag of bitterness on one shoulder,
over the other a sack of second guessing.
With one hand I drag along a load of discontent,
and with the other I hold to other burdens
that show up along the way.

We come to a fork in the path.
Jesus bids me to sit still at His feet.
I decide that I am exhausted and
resting at His feet just might be the answer.

As I sit there, I find myself filled with His peace and love;
forgiveness and grace pour down on me.

He looks at me with compassion and begins to speak.

Come to Me, for you are burdened,
I want to give you rest, rest for your soul.
I see you are loaded down with all this baggage that you
were never meant to carry.
Allow Me to carry your burdens.
You are missing the life I have for you
as you tote these things.
Many of these things are thrown over your shoulder
simply because you don't trust Me.
You want to take control of what you
were never meant to handle.

Aren't you so tired?

Let Me restore to you the joy of My salvation
and renew a steadfast spirit within you.
Allow Me to take your baggage.
Place your feet into My footprints.

Let's not wait until you hit rock bottom to sit and chat.
Sit at My feet often to gain your strength for the journey.
Nothing is too hard for Me, cast all your cares on Me,
I care so much for you.

When you get tired, let Me carry you.

The road will twist and turn.
The weather and seasons will change.
Some hills will be super steep, but if you stick close,
We can climb them together.

When you find yourself reaching for baggage
to throw over your shoulder, reach for Me instead.

I will be the whisper of truth.
I will give you new vision if you let Me take it all.
I will clear your view.

Are you ready to travel now?
It's time to go.

As we get up, He looks at me and glances at my bags.

Keep your eyes fixed on Me, don't let Me out of your sight.
Trust Me and I will lighten your load.
I promise I will never leave you.
I'm with you through it all.

1 Timothy 1:14, Psalm 51:12, Luke 10:39-41
Jeremiah 32:17, 1 Peter 5:7, Hebrews 12:2, Deuteronomy 31:6

COME AS YOU ARE

Come, see a man
who told me everything
I ever did.

John 4:29

COME AS YOU ARE

We were all gathered for a weekend retreat.
All heartbroken over our past, we were there
to find healing.

Upon arrival, you didn't have to ask why the other was
there, for everyone had fallen the same, there was no
hiding. In fact, I think we all found freedom in knowing we
were not alone. We came ready to confess our brokenness
to one another. We left never the same. (James 5:16)

I knew Jesus already, but, would He really forgive this part
of me? Had I been set free?
I came to the retreat kicking a little bit.
I left skipping, made new and changed forever.

I met His love in a different way this time.
He assured me there's no condemnation and He is mine,
As I voiced my heartache and deep regret.
I did this before others as I hadn't done yet.
Love filled the room. I admitted I had not been in His way.
I spilled out my grief and Jesus had so much to say.
I raised my hands in surrender.
It was as if I heard a shout.
I heard the birds louder and the sun came out.
There was a peace I hadn't known before like this.
My face turned toward the sun.
The breeze was His kiss.

The moment was love and the world stood still.
A butterfly touched me and He became so real.
I was set free and made new as the birds sang along.
Free and forgiven was the name of the song.
I whispered a prayer in deep gratitude and love.
Certain of His presence, compassion rained from above.
I admitted I was so broken and much afraid,
and He sang the refrain of the grace that He gave.

He knew my grief, my regret and my shame.
He assured me that He loves me and knows me by name.

Love's broken here. The road is bumpy and long.
There are good notes and bad notes in life's song.
He gave me a new song to sing on that day,
that He knows everything I ever did and loves me anyway.

"Come, see the man who told me everything I ever did."
(John 4:29)
See, His name is Jesus.
You see, He is faithful to forgive and cleanse us. (1 John 1:9)

Afraid to come like you are? Heartbroken and ashamed?
Know that you are not alone, we've all fallen, and lost and
broken is the only way to come.

Trust me. Trust Him. Come as you are – you will see!

GUARANTEED

"You are Sealed by the Holy Spirit
&
Marked as Christ's own forever."
(Ephesians 1:13)

I am marked with scars and a mess in restoration. His hands are marked with scars that cover mine. From my first breath to the present, His fingerprints can be traced in my life. I am a work in progress in the hands of a trustworthy God and "I am confident that He will continue His work and carry me home." (Philippians 1:6)

"It's in Christ that we find out who we are and what we are living for. Long before we first heard of Christ and got our hopes up, He had His eye on us, had designs on us for glorious living, part of the overall purpose He is working out in everything and everyone. It's in Christ that you, once you heard the message of truth and believed the gospel of your salvation, that you were marked in Him with the seal, the promised Holy Spirit, who is a deposit guaranteeing your inheritance, to God be all the praise and glory."
(Ephesians 1:11-14)

I hope we will meet again and turn more pages together as He continues to uncover His story of grace. But, most of all, I hope you meet and know Jesus.

Marked and Sealed,

Lori

THANKSGIVINGS

I will give thanks to You, Lord,
with all my herat;
I will tell of all Your
wonderful deeds.

Psalm 9:1

THANKSGIVINGS

The Lord is faithful to plant people in our lives. It was my "TTY" circle that first put this idea in motion. It had floated around in my heart, but they lovingly gave me the push to bring it in for a landing. TTY, "Through the Years," is what we call our group; lifelong friendships that continue to grow deeper as we delve into the true meaning of life.

Carol, Janine, Kristi, Tami: I am forever grateful for your sweet encouragement and love. You mean the world to me. Carol: You were much more than just my "assistant" to help with fonts and layout. You offered insights that I could not see.

Lisa: I penned you my "angel" since you flew into my life by surprise. Who knew you were an editor? You got first peeks at these pages and gave them wings.

Wendy: Olé friend, what a welcome surprise to be reunited. Wild story and not by chance. Your graphic design was the finishing touch and you carried it to the end.

Mom and Dad: You've always cheered me on, loved me through it all.

Gary: You got me over computer hurdles, but even more, you've always believed in me, my brother, my friend.

My dearest husband, Will: You've walked alongside me and supported me. I am so thankful for the Lord's hand in our marriage. He has done great things!

My dear children, Charlotte Anne and William: You have taught me so many things in life, the Lord has used you to grow me. I'm still always learning. I love you to the moon and back. You are two of my greatest gifts from the Lord. You light up my life.

Faye: You faithfully served and taught me His Word for so many years, increasing my hunger to know Him. It forever changed my course.

Tuck: You poured into my early years and planted seeds that were watered by the Lord and grew. You introduced me to Jesus. I am forever thankful.

Give thanks to the LORD, for He is good;
His love endures forever.

Psalm 107:1

Made in the USA
Middletown, DE
01 August 2019